DIVERSITY ON THE JOB

DIVERSITY ON THE JOB: THE IMPORTANCE OF DIVERSITY AND THE CHANGING WORKPLACE

Imagine an organization where everyone is the same. People have the same opinions. They're all close in age. Their backgrounds are similar. They even have the same political and religious beliefs. Would you want to work there?

Of course, such a company probably doesn't exist in real life. And even if it did, few people would want to work there.

Diversity makes things interesting. Interacting with people who offer fresh new perspectives can teach you how to broaden your horizons and find creative ways to solve problems.

A diverse workplace can even help you identify new markets, products, or business opportunities. Diverse groups are less likely to get stuck in routines and groupthink. In other words, diversity is good for business!

Because diversity is so important, understanding it is crucial, not just for the HR Department, but for anyone who works in a modern global company.

This course outlines the importance of diversity in the workplace:

You'll discover how the concept of diversity is constantly changing and the resulting myths surrounding it.

You'll also find out how diversity can benefit not only your organization, but you as an individual.

Finally, the course discusses some of the challenges and barriers to diversity in the workplace and ways you can overcome them.

Developing diversity isn't always easy, but the benefits far outweigh the effort required. If your company wants to achieve success in the changing marketplace and explore new sources of competitive advantage, diversity should be one of its priorities.

DISPELLING THE MYTHS ABOUT DIVERSITY IN THE WORKPLACE

Myths about diversity
If you asked ten people what the word diversity means, you'd probably get ten different answers. That's because diversity is a concept that's constantly evolving. It's not easy to define, and everyone has a different idea of what diversity actually means.

Reflect
You probably have your own ideas or assumptions about what diversity means. What comes to mind when you think about diversity in the workplace?

Because people have such different ideas about diversity, many myths and misunderstandings about it still exist. You may even have included some of these myths in your comments on the previous page. This topic will cover three of the most common myths: diversity is all about differences of race and gender, diversity is all about equal opportunities, and diversity is an HR issue.

Diversity: not just race and gender
The first myth – that **diversity is all about race and gender** – is perhaps the most pervasive. Consider Bill, who manages the Accounting Department at his company. He takes special pride in

the
diversity of his group, which includes different ages, sexes, and cultural backgrounds.

To Bill, these broad categories of gender and race are what diversity is all about. Do you agree?

There's no question that any definition of diversity must include race and gender. But, you should keep in mind that not all diversities are visible.

Think about it – every day, you're constantly exposed to diversity, even if you don't realize it.

People can be diverse even in terms of invisible attributes. For instance, in any group you'll find different thoughts, values, social backgrounds, and levels of education.

Other invisible attributes contributing to diversity can include your generation, sexual orientation, marital status, political or religious beliefs, physical abilities, and life experience.

When you consider the fact that there's more to people than just the way they look on the outside, it becomes clear why diversity means more than race and gender. Those invisible attributes contribute a great deal to the mix of ideas and perspectives in the workplace. So, when you think about your own workplace, do you now perceive it in a new light? It's probably a more diverse place than you thought!

Diversity: not just equal opportunity

Another myth about diversity is that it's **all about equal opportunities**. Yes, providing employment equity is one aspect of diversity in the workplace, but diversity encompasses more than just that.

Question
What do you think are some other aspects of diversity in the workplace?
Options:
1. Helping people from different backgrounds learn to work together effectively

2. Fostering an inclusive culture that values the contribution of a workforce made of diverse individuals
   3. Avoiding monoculture and accepting, understanding, and adapting to differences
   4. Realizing that equal opportunity programs are only in place because employers are required to use them
   5. Assuming that all workers in an organization have similar needs and are working toward meeting those needs

Answer
Other aspects of diversity in the workplace include helping people from different backgrounds to work together effectively, fostering an inclusive culture that values the contribution of a workforce made of diverse individuals, and avoiding monoculture.

Correct answer(s):
1. Helping people from different backgrounds learn to work together effectively
2. Fostering an inclusive culture that values the contribution of a workforce made of diverse individuals
3. Avoiding monoculture and accepting, understanding, and adapting to differences

In companies that have developed diversity far beyond just equal opportunities, you'll notice three things: people from different backgrounds are helped and encouraged to work together; the contribution of a workforce made of diverse individuals is valued; and finally, monoculture is avoided and differences among individuals are understood, recognized, and accepted.
See each concept to learn more about it.

People are encouraged to work together
Diversity in the workplace entails finding ways to help people from different backgrounds – social or economic, for instance – be productive as a team.

Diverse contributions are valued
Workplaces must focus on creating a culture that values every-

one's contribution, not just the contributions of a few people or groups.

Monoculture is avoided

Avoiding monoculture – which is characterized by homogeneity – is a huge part of diversity in the workplace. Very few companies could be successful without the different perspectives their diverse workforces provide.

The key thing to remember is that diversity is about focusing on the big picture, not just pieces of it. Think of it this way. Suppose you have a box of green balls. Now, add a few red balls, and perhaps three blue ones. The red and blue balls represent diversity, right? Well, not exactly. The diversity is actually represented by the entire mixture: green, red, and blue.

Diversity in the workplace is no different. Each person, as an individual, doesn't represent diversity.

Instead, the entire mixture of individuals – with their unique ideas and experiences – is the real diversity in an organization.

Diversity: not just an HR issue

Now move on to the final myth about diversity – that **it's an HR issue**. Many people, perhaps yourself included, think of HR when they hear the word diversity. However, the reality is that diversity isn't just an organizational issue created by the HR Department. It actually starts with you, as an individual. Being exposed to diversity broadens your perspectives and might even enhance your creativity and problem- solving abilities.

When people have different views and backgrounds, they often observe a problem from different perspectives. This can help broaden their views and the way they approach problems.

See each employee for an example of how two people can approach a problem from different perspectives.

Victoria

"Recently, we had a new person join our team. William is fluent in Spanish, so he can take on clients that some of our English-speaking team members can't. When William joined the team, I felt like he was taking new clients away from the rest of us."

Taku

"When Victoria told me her concerns about William, I helped her see that he's actually an asset to our team. Before he arrived, we didn't have anyone who could speak Spanish – now we have someone who can increase our client base. Not only that, but William also has great networking skills and brought a large clientele with him to our company."

When Taku showed Victoria how William wasn't a hindrance but a benefit to the team, she saw the situation differently.

By viewing things from Taku's perspective, Victoria was able to broaden her viewpoint and realize that diversity can actually help her team flourish.

Some companies bypass the HR Department altogether by including diversity in their strategic vision. For example, consider a company that emphasizes and encourages differences instead of suppressing them. This allows fresh ideas to emerge. Instead of forcing everyone to think along the same lines, the company focuses on the varied perspectives that emerge when differences are celebrated. This approach provides the company with business advantages not enjoyed by its peers who don't foster diversity.

By clearing away the myths about diversity in the workplace, you'll be able to focus on the ways diversity can benefit your organization and you as an individual.

Reflect

Now that you've learned about some of the myths surrounding diversity in the workplace, have your beliefs and assumptions changed?

Question

Which statements about diversity in the workplace are correct?

Options:
1. The concept of workplace diversity includes differences of thought and values

2. Fostering workplace diversity encourages people from different backgrounds to work together effectively
3. Companies that foster workplace diversity work to create an inclusive culture that values the contribution of a diverse workforce
4. Workplace diversity is about encouraging monoculture
5. Workplace diversity puts companies on an equal playing field with their peers who don't encourage diversity

Answer

Option 1: *This option is correct. Not all diversities are visible in the way that race and gender are. People can be diverse even in terms of invisible attributes, such as differences of thought and values.*

Option 2: *This option is correct. Fostering diversity in the workplace entails finding ways to help people from different backgrounds – social or economic, for instance – be productive as a team.*

Option 3: *This option is correct. Workplaces should focus on creating a culture that values everyone's contribution, not just the contribution of a few people.*

Option 4: *This option is incorrect. Actually, avoiding monoculture – which is characterized by homogeneity – is a huge part of diversity in the workplace. Very few companies could be successful without the different perspectives diversity provides.*

Option 5: *This option is incorrect. When companies include diversity in their strategic vision it*
can provide them with business advantages not enjoyed by peers who don't foster diversity.

Summary

Because people have such different ideas about diversity, many myths and misunderstandings about it still exist: that diversity is all about race and gender, that diversity is all about equal opportunities, and that diversity is an HR issue.

By clearing away the myths about diversity in the workplace, you'll be able to focus on the ways diversity can benefit your organization and you as an individual.

HOW DIVERSITY BENEFITS ORGANIZATIONS AND EMPLOYEES

How organizations deal with diversity

Think about your workplace for a moment. The people you work with probably come from different backgrounds and have different opinions and beliefs. How does each individual add value to your company? What perspectives do you and your colleagues contribute as a result of your diversity? And how does having a diverse workforce impact your company?

Globalization has resulted in modern workplaces being increasingly diverse. Social groups and ethnicities that were traditionally excluded from some types of roles have increasingly entered the labor market or taken on new roles.

To respond to these global changes, both managers and employees are having to become more aware of the value of embracing diversity in the workplace.

But why should your company care about diversity? Does investing in diversity really have an impact on your organization?

In short, yes it does. Many companies are starting to realize the benefits of embracing diversity. The ways they address diversity vary greatly from company to company, but they typically fall into four broad categories: welcome aboard, fit in, don't rock the boat, and help us achieve our goals.

See each of the different ways companies address diversity to learn more about it.

Welcome aboard
This is the most common way companies address diversity and is what many people think of when they hear the word. Essentially, it involves inclusion – having employees from a variety of cultures, backgrounds, races, and genders.

Fit in
This approach involves denying that differences exist. Companies demonstrate this when they assure employees that differences are meaningless – the only thing that matters is performance.

This way of dealing with diversity is based on the belief that, over time, employees who are in the minority will eventually learn to become more like those who are in the majority.

Don't rock the boat
When companies use this approach, they encourage people to suppress their differences. Sometimes they'll isolate people with differences – for instance, by creating groups comprised of employees from the same racial group or culture. Other companies may also work at building relationships between different people and groups, but they encourage them to find similarities and minimize their differences.

This approach involves tolerating differences – basically allowing them to exist without either valuing or demeaning them.

Help us achieve our goals
This approach involves employees working together toward mutual goals. It's the ideal way for companies to address diversity, but it's a relatively new concept for many companies. With this approach, the company encourages employees to understand, accept, and value differences.

This takes some effort on everyone's part, but accommodating diversity in its entirety can go farther than any of the other methods toward helping a company achieve its goals.

Question

Victoria's company has recently changed the way it deals with diversity. In the past, managers insisted that every employee was the same, regardless of background. But now, managers welcome differences, realizing that each individual has unique talents to offer.

Is this the ideal way for Victoria's company to deal with diversity?

Options:

1. Yes 2. No

Answer

Actually, Victoria's company is encouraging employees to help it achieve its goals by helping them understand and accept differences. It's the ideal way for companies to address diversity, but is a relatively new concept for many companies.

Benefits of developing diversity

Companies may use many different methods to deal with diversity. But no matter which method your company may use, developing diversity should be at the top of your corporate agenda. By effectively leveraging the differences among employees and developing diversity, your company can benefit in four areas:

employee retention, which includes low turnover, increased productivity, job satisfaction

creativity, by making the best use of employees' abilities and tapping into a broader range of talents

conflict management, by increasing the ability to handle conflicts productively, and

corporate image, with the aim of developing a reputation as a desirable place to work

Almost every company has dealt with employee turnover at one time or another. The first benefit of developing diversity is improved **employee retention**, which translates into low turnover and improved performance.

When your company develops and practices diversity, employees tend to be more appreciative and respectful of individual differences and similarities. They feel they're given equal opportunities and are valued and treated with respect and fairness. And they appreciate benefits and initiatives meant to promote diversity. The result? Higher morale, more job satisfaction, and increased productivity.

One of the ways a company can promote diversity is to ensure that it's family friendly.

Family friendliness allows equal opportunities for people with families so that employees can make work compatible with their own private lives without sacrificing opportunities for career progression.

Jorge is a single father who is climbing the corporate ladder. Follow along as he speaks with his manager Victor.

Jorge: Hi Victor. Would it be alright if I leave early tomorrow? I need to take my daughter to an appointment.

Victor: Sure Jorge, that's no problem at all.

Jorge: Thanks Victor. I really appreciate your being flexible.

Victor: Well, we're serious about giving employees the flexibility they need. Whether it's occasionally working from home, or leaving early sometimes, I hope you know we'll accommodate you the best we can.

Jorge: And that's just one of the reasons I love working here!

Jorge is very satisfied with his company, which fosters diversity by giving single parents the same opportunities as everyone else. Jorge plans to work there for a long time. This benefits his company because it won't lose a valuable employee like Jorge – it's a win-win situation.

The second benefit to companies that develop diversity is that they can **make the best use of employees' creativity and tap into a broader range of talents**. Your company might be uncertain about whether diversity will actually benefit it because the outcome can't be predicted. However, developing diversity can have several different outcomes.

Question
What do you think are potential outcomes of developing diversity?

Options:
1. Increased creativity
2. Better problem solving
3. Improved ability to identify and define new markets or products 4. Fresh perspectives
5. A similar viewpoint among all employees
6. Improved ability to assimilate with the rest of the workforce

Answer

Potential outcomes of developing diversity include increased creativity, better problem solving, improved ability to identify and define new markets or products, and fresh perspectives.

It makes sense that a group of people from a wide range of backgrounds would have increased creativity and problem-solving skills. There's also a greater chance that new markets and products will be identified. And a broader range of talents means fresh perspectives that can help your company succeed.

For example, a magazine publisher is trying to increase its circulation numbers. A diverse staff of writers would be more likely to have enough interesting ideas to make the magazine a success than a more homogenous staff. The magazine publisher should consider tapping into a wide range of talents to appeal to the broadest audience possible.

Question

How can your company use diversity to increase group creativity?

Options:
1. By making use of a wide pool of talent
2. By ensuring the group is made up entirely of people with visible differences 3. By asking for input from only one or two group members

Answer

Option 1: *This is the correct option. Your company should make the best use of employees' abilities and tap into a broader range of talents. A group of people from a wide range of backgrounds will have in-*

creased creativity and problem-solving skills.

Option 2: This option is incorrect. When a group is made up entirely of people with more visible differences, such as gender and age, the group's creativity can be hindered.

Option 3: This option is incorrect. To increase group creativity, the group should be made up of people from a wide range of backgrounds. A broader range of talents means fresh perspectives that can help your company succeed.

Moving on, the third way companies benefit from developing diversity is that employees have an **increased ability to handle intellectual conflict productively**. As with creativity, visible diversity tends to cause people to be able to handle conflict better than those in groups where diversity isn't evident.

That's because visible differences are a cue to group members that conflict is likely to happen, which means they're more prepared to deal with divergences.

Over time, the group learns to handle conflict better than a more homogenous group, because people aren't surprised when differences of opinion emerge.

Imagine that three teams are working on the same project. One is comprised of five men, one is comprised of five women, and the other is comprised of a mixture of men and women.

It's possible that the team made up of both genders may expect some conflict. Men and women can have different ideas and do things differently.

Because the team members are prepared for conflict, they won't be surprised when differences emerge. They may have a better chance of dealing with the conflict productively than the groups made up entirely of the same gender.

Question
Why do teams with a high level of diversity have an increased ability to handle conflict productively?
Options:
1. Team members are more prepared to deal with divergences that emerge

2. The conflict takes team members by surprise and their main concern is eliminating the conflict
3. Teams with a high level of diversity don't experience conflict
4. Team members are too focused on overcoming their differences to have many conflicts

Answer

Option 1: *This is the correct option. In groups where diversity is more visible, people may see differences as a cue that conflict is likely to happen, which means they can be more prepared to deal with divergences.*

Option 2: *This option is incorrect. A group with a high level of diversity can learn to handle conflict better than a more homogenous group because people aren't surprised when differences of opinion emerge.*

Option 3: *This option is incorrect. All groups experience conflict at one time or another. But in groups where diversity is more visible, people tend to be able to handle conflict better because visible differences are a cue to group members that conflict can happen. They're more prepared to deal with divergences.*

Option 4: *This option is incorrect. In groups where diversity is more visible, people tend to be able to handle conflict better than those in groups where diversity isn't evident. The visible differences are a cue that conflict can happen, which means they're more prepared to deal with divergences.*

Reflect

A final benefit of developing diversity is that it can positively impact your **company's corporate image**. How do you think a company's image can be enhanced by diversity?

You may have said that diversity makes your company more desirable. Companies that work at developing diversity are often known as being employers of choice. Because they have a wide range of talent, they're frequently listed among the top ten or twenty employers. This, in turn, helps them attract even more talent, since people are drawn to companies that are known for being great employers.

DIVERSITY ON THE JOB

Developing diversity can take time and effort, and your company might be unsure if it's worthwhile.

However, by putting in the work and making diversity a priority, your organization can enjoy enormous gains and reap the benefits you learned about in this topic.

But your company isn't the only one that benefits from diversity. You, as an individual, can benefit as well. When your company develops diversity, you'll be exposed to new ideas. This means you'll likely become more open minded and learn how to think outside the box.

Question

What are the potential benefits to a company that develops diversity in the workplace?

Options:

1. Employees are more productive and have higher job satisfaction
2. The company can tap into a broader range of talents
3. Employees are more prepared for conflict to emerge and are better able to deal with it
4. The company has a better chance of being viewed as a desirable place to work
5. The company doesn't have to worry about following employment standards since it's hiring a diverse workforce
6. Employees never have to deal with conflict because it rarely emerges where diversity is present

Answer

Option 1: *This option is correct. One of the benefits of developing diversity is improved employee retention, which translates into low turnover, improved performance, and higher job satisfaction.*

Option 2: *This option is correct. Companies that develop diversity can make the best use of employees' abilities and tap into a broader range of talents. A group of people from a wide range of backgrounds will have increased creativity and problem-solving skills, which benefits the company.*

Option 3: *This option is correct. In groups where diversity is more visible, people tend to be able to handle conflict better than those in groups where diversity isn't evident. Visible differences can be a cue to group members that conflict can happen, which means they're more prepared to deal with divergences.*

Option 4: *This option is correct. Companies that work at developing diversity are often known as being employers of choice. Because they have a wide range of talent, they're frequently listed among the top ten or twenty employers.*

Option 5: *This option is incorrect. Regardless of whether or not a company encourages diversity, it still needs to follow employment standards.*

Option 6: *This option is incorrect. Conflict can't always be avoided but can be managed or diminished over time as group members learn about each other's differences.*

Question
In what ways do you think working in a diverse organization would benefit you as an employee?
Options:
1. You'll be exposed to new ideas
2. You'll be able to think outside the box
3. You'll become more open minded
4. You'll be able to let others do the creative work 5. You'll have a better chance of being promoted
Answer

Option 1: *This option is correct. Diversity can expose you to new ideas that may result in different ways of solving business problems.*

Option 2: *This option is correct. Being exposed to different ideas, cultures, and points of view can help you think outside the box instead of doing things the same way you've always done them.*

Option 3: *This option is correct. Working in a diverse environment can help you become more open minded and understanding of the value all people bring to an organization.*

Option 4: *This option is incorrect. Although a diverse workforce often brings about more creativity, you'll still have to put in your share of* *work to be seen as a team player.*

Option 5: *This option is incorrect. Whether your company encourages diversity or not, the only way to be promoted is through hard work.*

Summary

To respond to modern global changes, managers have become more aware of the value of embracing diversity in the workplace. Many companies are starting to realize the benefits of embracing diversity.

Effectively developing diversity can benefit your company in four areas. The first benefit is improved employee retention, which translates into low turnover and improved performance. The second benefit is that your company can make the best use of employees' creativity and tap into a broader range of talents. The third benefit is that employees have an increased ability to handle intellectual conflict productively. Finally, the fourth benefit is that diversity can positively impact your company's corporate image.

CHALLENGES AND BARRIERS TO DIVERSITY

Barriers to diversity
Diversity can be a tough issue for organizations to deal with. Although many companies want to foster diversity, they often encounter barriers and challenges along the way to establishing and developing diversity in the workplace.

Reflect
What do you think are some challenges your own company might need to overcome in order to foster diversity?

Every company is different, but most encounter a few common barriers to diversity. Your answer might have included some of these: all types of prejudice and stereotypes, cultural expectations, jealousy and defensiveness, and resistance to change.

Prejudice and stereotypes
The first barrier to diversity involves **prejudice and stereotypes**, which can lead to discrimination and unequal opportunities. Prejudices of all types are still the biggest barrier to most companies' efforts to develop diversity. Most people, perhaps yourself included, think they're fair. You don't consciously judge people based on race, age, or gender. But prejudice is often unconscious, which is why it's so difficult to overcome.
So what exactly is prejudice? Essentially, it's perpetuating negative stereotypes instead of accepting differences.

Prejudice within the workplace is especially challenging because it can cause barriers to develop for some employees. It can separate information from the people who need it most and prevent them from obtaining the resources they require to get ahead in their careers. Many find it difficult to balance career with family life, and a lack of skills can make it hard to get the promotions they want. And diversity can create fault lines that divide groups instead of encouraging them to embrace differences.
See each barrier to learn more about it.

Lack of resources
Many employees struggle to get the experience and development opportunities needed to compete for senior positions.

Balancing career and family
It can be difficult for some employees to find a balance between their work and personal lives. This is especially true for women and men who are the primary caregivers for their children.

Lack of skills
It's common for some employees and managers to lack certain skills – political or corporate skills, for instance. This can make them feel uncomfortable, which hinders their chances of success.

Fault lines
In general, people are more comfortable dealing with others who are similar to them. A diverse workforce can enhance creativity, but it can also create fault lines that split a group into subgroups. For instance, a group made up of three men in their twenties and three men in their sixties may encounter more conflict than a group made up of men of similar ages.

So what can you, as an individual, do to overcome prejudice and stereotypes? Well, for one thing, you can become aware of your own biases, assumptions, and social and racial prejudices.
By questioning yourself, you can figure out if you're acting on assumptions or facts.
Maria and Victor are employees of the same sporting goods company. When their company began to develop diversity, they both

realized they held unconscious prejudices.
See the employees to learn more about their prejudices.

Maria
"When my company hired George and he was placed on my team, I was really annoyed. He looks like he's about 70 years old, and I wondered how anyone so old could possibly do a good job. But George is one of our most productive team members, and I realized I held a prejudice that older people don't make good employees. I was wrong."

Victor
"I've always said I believe that men and women should be equal, but when my company hired a woman to run my department, I realized I didn't actually believe it at all! I was angry at first – why couldn't they have hired a man who could actually do the job? But Layla is an amazing manager, and I'm trying not to stereotype people anymore."

Question
Now, recall what you've learned about prejudice and stereotypes. How can prejudice hinder diversity?
Options:
1. It can be the basis for discrimination and unequal opportunities
2. It can cause people to become ambivalent about differences
3. It can mean extra barriers for all employees
4. It can lead to employees who are part of minority groups getting all the desirable management positions

Answer
Option 1: *This is the correct option. Prejudice can hinder diversity because it can cause people to discriminate based on their stereotypes about certain groups. This can lead to unequal opportunities being provided to the groups being discriminated against.*
Option 2: *This option is incorrect. Actually, prejudice causes people to view differences as deficiencies, not become ambivalent about them.*

This can hinder a company's diversity efforts.
Option 3: *This option is incorrect. Prejudice is especially challenging because it can create even more barriers for some employees who are part of a minority group.*
Option 4: *This option is incorrect. Some employees who are part of minority groups struggle to get the experience and development opportunities needed to compete for senior positions, which can hinder a company's efforts to develop diversity.*

Cultural expectations

The second barrier to diversity involves **cultural expectations**. In general, people who come from different cultural backgrounds have different expectations about management styles, work rules, and even appropriate behavior. When expectations among group members differ, it can have a negative impact on the group's cohesion.

It's crucial that a group can communicate effectively about values, objectives, and tasks. But cultural expectations can make it difficult for group members to come to any sort of agreement about these issues, and this can eventually destroy the team.

If your company wants to avoid these negative consequences, it must figure out a way to manage cultural differences. This is where the challenge lies. Often, some employees find their ideas and opinions dismissed in favor of the more dominant point of view.

To be successful, your company needs to determine how to create a model of success that incorporates diversity instead of forcing all employees to fit into traditional ideas and visions. Even though many employees tend to accept the dominant culture, it's important that your company find a way to incorporate the cultural differences.

Question
Now think about your own role in overcoming cultural expectations. How would you rate your ability to deal with cultural differences?

Options:
1. I'm never sure how to relate to people from different cultures 2. I'm somewhat friendly with people from different cultures
3. I love finding out about people from different cultures

Answer

Option 1: *Many people aren't sure how to relate to people from different cultures, especially if they've only been exposed to homogenous groups. But taking the time to learn more about your coworkers can help you communicate better, which improves your team's cohesion.*

Option 2: *To overcome cultural expectations, it's important to try to learn more about your coworkers. Knowing why people think the way they do, for instance, can be helpful when it comes time to make team decisions – you won't be so quick to blame differences of opinion solely on cultural differences.*

Option 3: *Asking questions to learn more about people from different backgrounds is one of the best ways to overcome cultural expectations. When you know more about why people think or behave the way they do, you'll be better able to communicate and work through disagreements.*

As an individual, you can take actions to overcome cultural expectations. You can improve your intercultural literacy by getting to know your colleagues' cultures and differences.

By talking about expectations openly, you replace judgments with curiosity. This will help you connect with your coworkers and better understand their behavior.

Question

Now you know that people from different cultures tend to have different expectations in terms of authority, work rules, and behavior.

How can this hinder diversity?

Options:
1. It can create problems of communication and understanding within the organization
2. It can negatively affect the cohesion of workgroups

3. It can lead to a company forcing all employees to accept the dominant culture
   4. It can create fault lines that divide teams

Answer

Option 1: *This option is correct. Cultural expectations can make it difficult for group members to communicate effectively and understand each other, and this can eventually destroy the team.*

Option 2: *This option is correct. When expectations among group members differ, it can have a negative impact on the group's cohesion.*

Option 3: *This option is incorrect. Even though many employees tend to accept the dominant culture, this shouldn't be by force on the part of the company.*

Option 4: *This option is incorrect. Actually, prejudice and stereotypes – not cultural expectations – create fault lines that can divide teams.*

Jealousy and defensiveness

People often feel threatened when they think their advantages will be taken away. That's why the third barrier to diversity is **jealousy and defensiveness**. If your company doesn't encourage and embrace diversity properly, employees who have traditionally been advantaged might feel that these advantages are being threatened.

For example, employees who have traditionally been handed promotions might feel resentful that they now have to compete for those jobs. This can lead to jealousy and defensiveness – both of which can negatively impact your team's productivity.

Jealousy and defensiveness are most likely to become issues when diversity is forced. If employees are made to work with people they normally wouldn't socialize with, they may feel they need to change their behavior – which, over time, leads to resentment.

It can be difficult for you, as an individual, to overcome this barrier. It's natural to be jealous or defensive when you feel threatened. But by becoming a "diversity advocate," you can get past these negative feelings. Try bridging differences and building understanding, or discussing diversity openly. Instead of viewing diversity as negative, try to find the positive aspects.

Question

How can jealousy and defensiveness be a barrier to a company trying to develop diversity?

Options:

1. Employees who have traditionally been advantaged might feel threatened
2. The company will have to give promotions based on seniority to avoid jealousy 3. Some employees will have to stop competing for jobs

Answer

Option 1: This is the correct option. Employees who may have traditionally been handed promotions might feel resentful that they now have to compete for those jobs. This can lead to jealousy and defensiveness, which can negatively impact a company.

Option 2: This option is incorrect. Regardless of whether a company is developing diversity, promotions should be given on merit, not to try to avoid jealousy.

Option 3: This option is incorrect. Diversity means that everyone in a company should have the same opportunities. Anyone with the required skills can compete for jobs, whether they're traditionally advantaged employees or not.

Resistance

No matter how much enthusiasm your company has for diversity and how much effort it puts into developing diversity, it might still encounter **resistance**, which is the final barrier to diversity. Resistance can happen for two reasons: some people feel there's no need to change, while others just can't understand the benefits of developing diversity.

See each reason for resistance to learn more about it.

No need to change

It's common for some employees, especially executives, to feel that there's no need to change because the company is successful just the way it is. They believe the culture should stay the same, even if the current structure might not be working.

It can be difficult to overcome this resistance, but it's worthwhile to put in the effort. Those in opposition need to be convinced that the traditional way of doing things isn't going to help the company get ahead – even if things seem to be going along just fine.

Can't understand the benefits

Some executives have a difficult time understanding the benefits of diversity. They tend to think in terms of profit versus social responsibility – and profit wins out. It's not that they don't believe in social and ethical responsibilities, it's just that they can't see how diversity can offer measurable financial gain. This means resistance to investing in diversity initiatives because the benefits of doing so are vague.

Overcoming this obstacle is possible, but only when the organization has clearly defined its objectives with regard to diversity. The company must show executives how the expected payoffs of developing diversity are worth achieving.

In Taku's company, which is a large software developer, managers have always been Caucasian males in their fifties or sixties. No one has ever questioned this – and up until now, it seems to have worked just fine. But in the past year, things have changed. Profits have been falling, and the company's key software product hasn't been doing well on the market.

Follow along as Taku and his supervisor, Julia, discuss the problem.

Taku: I just came from the sales meeting. Did you know our profits have dropped 42% in the last year?

Julia: Really? 42%? What is management planning on doing about it?

Taku: Well, from what I understand, not much! They seem to think things will turn around next quarter, but I'm not so sure.

Julia: That's the problem in this company. Management thinks things should stay the same, even though the economy is chan-

ging.
We need to stay relevant!

Taku: I couldn't agree more. When was the last time we came out with a new product? Or used a different marketing strategy?

Julia: Not since I've been working here. Things haven't changed much in the four years since I joined the company.

Taku: Well, unless things do change, I fear we'll be searching for new jobs in the very near future!

Taku and Julia are experiencing resistance in their company. Managers don't want to change the way things are done, even though the company's profits are suffering. But if things don't change, their company probably won't survive.

Overcoming resistance might seem like an impossible task for you as an individual. But think about how you learn to accept any change – you focus on the benefits. If you focus on the benefits of diversity instead of thinking of all the reasons it might not work, you'll probably find the resistance becomes less of an issue over time.

Overcoming the barriers to diversity isn't always easy. In fact, it can seem like an insurmountable task that's not worth the work required.

But if your company puts in the effort and overcomes these challenges, it can reap the benefits of a diverse workforce.

Question

Why do some organizations experience resistance to developing diversity?

Options:
1. Some employees think they don't need to change as they're already successful
2. Some employees find it hard to understand the financial payoffs of implementing and developing diversity in the workplace
3. Some employees are resentful of newcomers who compete for available jobs

4. Some employees think that developing diversity is too much work

Answer

Option 1: *This option is correct. It's common for some employees to feel there's no need to change because the company is successful just the way it is. They believe the culture should stay the same, even if the current structure might not be working.*

Option 2: *This option is correct. Some employees, including some executives, have a difficult time understanding the benefits of diversity. They tend to think in terms of profit versus social responsibility – and profit wins out. This means resistance to investing in diversity initiatives because the benefits of doing so are vague.*

Option 3: *This option is incorrect. Actually, resentment leads to a different barrier to diversity – jealousy and defensiveness – not resistance.*

Option 4: *This option is incorrect. Although some employees might feel like diversity takes too much work, this isn't one of the causes of resistance.*

Summary

Diversity is a tough issue for many organizations to deal with. Companies want to foster diversity, but they often encounter barriers and challenges along the way to establishing and developing diversity in the workplace.

The most common barriers to diversity are prejudice and stereotypes, cultural expectations, jealousy and defensiveness, and resistance to change. Overcoming these barriers will help your organization become a leader in its industry.

DIVERSITY ON THE JOB: DIVERSITY AND YOU

In today's global economy, people of all ages, races, religions, cultures, and backgrounds work together – in the same work environments and across worldwide electronic networks.

And with the availability of a much larger talent pool, nearly all organizations are working to harness the promise of diversity – that increased creativity and synergy are forged when people of differing talents, ideas, and backgrounds work together.

But diversity comes with problems too. Whether you're dealing with a teammate from another country or a client with a different educational background, communications are complicated. Misunderstandings and frustrations are the order of the day when people from different backgrounds apply their own behavioral standards and expectations to each other.

For you to succeed in a diverse environment, you must be able to work well with others who aren't like you. The three topics in this course deal with three different aspects of diversity: Self-awareness and Diversity, Embracing Diversity, and Communicating in a Diverse Setting.

Select each topic to learn more about what it contains.

Self-awareness and Diversity

The first topic presents the importance of self-awareness in succeeding in a diverse environment. You'll learn about some tips for determining your core values, core beliefs, and biases, as well as for taking control of your self-talk.

Embracing Diversity
The second topic presents some methods you can use to work successfully with people from different backgrounds. Methods include developing a nuanced world view and investigating the rationale for behaviors that may seem strange to you. This topic also covers actions you can take to become a diversity advocate.

Communicating in a Diverse Setting
The third topic presents some techniques for communicating effectively to ensure your message gets across to people who may communicate very differently than you do.

Diversity is important – and it's becoming more important by the day. Take to heart what you learn in this course. By embracing diversity, you're preparing for the future.

SELF-AWARENESS AND DIVERSITY

Looking inward

When was the last opportunity you had to spend some time with yourself, developing your abilities and knowledge? Well, embracing diversity requires that you journey inward to gain awareness of how you think and feel so that you can begin to understand your cultural makeup.

In return for taking the sometimes long and difficult journey inward, you'll be well rewarded:

you'll be able to understand and manage your own feelings and reactions to diversity and differences, and

you'll be able to challenge and reverse any irrational, negative beliefs and assumptions that you may hold about your colleagues

Your ability to deal with diversity depends as much on what you know as on what you do. First, you must gain knowledge of your core values, core beliefs, and biases. Then you can take action to change what you don't like about your behaviors and challenge negative beliefs that you have about yourself and others.

Your core values

Think about these questions: Who are you? What do you stand for? What's important to you in life? What gives you joy? These questions are a good starting point for learning about yourself.

And self-awareness is crucial when you work with people from diverse backgrounds. If you're to build trust and connections with others, you must know who you are, what motivates you, what your expectations are, and what shapes those expectations. The key areas to examine in your journey to self-awareness are your core values, core beliefs, and biases.

Values are principles that define you. They determine your thinking about what's good or bad, right or wrong, and fair or unfair. If you are to understand how you behave and communicate in the world, you need to know what your values are.

Question
First of all, do you recognize what these qualities are?
The qualities are fairness, honesty, ambition, courage, challenge, money, self-development, tolerance, peace, competition, belonging, family, and recognition.
Options:
1. Values
2. Noble virtues
3. Motivational techniques
Answer
Option 1: *Right. These terms are all values – qualities that define who you are and what you want, deep down. Becoming self-aware requires you to know your values.*
Option 2: *Not all of them are noble. The pursuit of money isn't always noble, is it? Yet money – and all these other terms – are values. Becoming self-aware requires you to know your values.*
Option 3: *Actually, these things can motivate you, but they're not really techniques. These qualities are values.*

To determine your values, you can follow a series of steps: identify values that seem important, choose your core values, think about how you demonstrate your core values, and determine how to change actions or behaviors to demonstrate values you want to achieve.
See each step to learn more.

dentify values that seem important
Ask yourself, What gives me joy and fulfillment? What are the traits I admire in my role models and want to emulate? What traits are important to my family, to my peer group, and to my

country, ethnic group, and culture?

Choose your core values

Go over your list of values. Choose the five or six most important ones and arrange them in order of importance. These are your core values.

Think about how you demonstrate core values

Think about how you apply your core values in your work and your life. For instance, if family is a core value, do you make it a priority to spend quality time with family members every day?

Determine how to change actions or behaviors

If you don't demonstrate any one of your core values in your daily life, determine how to change your actions or behaviors to incorporate the value.

Your core beliefs

In addition to knowing your core values, you need to be aware of your **core beliefs**. Core beliefs are deeply held truths about yourself and your life. They're not universal truths, but truths as you believe them to be.

For example, do any of these core beliefs resonate with you?

"My work is a joyful experience."

"I'm a good person."

"I can't trust anyone, not even my family." "Why try? I always mess up anyway."

Positive core beliefs – such as "I'm a good person" – smooth interactions with other people because positive feelings easily spread to others. On the other hand, negative core beliefs paint the world in very dark colors. They result in divisiveness, depression, and poor interactions with other people.

Core beliefs often have their roots in childhood experiences. So to identify your core beliefs, go to the source and examine the formative elements in your upbringing – your family, peers, educational experiences, and cultural context.

See each element to learn some questions you can ask to examine the influences on your own core beliefs.

Family
What kind of messages did your parents and relatives communicate to you about yourself and other people?
Peers
What kind of attitudes and opinions did your peers have about you, your family, and diverse people?
Educational experience
Did your education prepare you to refute stereotypes and think independently?
Cultural context
How did your cultural background affect your thinking and attitudes about the world and diverse people?

Awareness of your core beliefs can lead to change. It may not be easy – core beliefs are deeply ingrained in the psyche; yet it's important to try. You want to be able to live with passion, energy, and gratitude, rather than isolation, depression, and gloom.

Question
Which actions should you take to gain awareness of your own core values and core beliefs?
Options:
1. Identify the traits you admire in your role models
2. Identify influences your family had on your thinking and attitudes
3. Determine how your cultural context influenced you to think and behave in a certain way
4. Identify the role your peers played in shaping your attitudes and behaviors
5. Determine how to turn negative core beliefs into positive ones
6. Raise your children in a way that fosters the formation of positive core beliefs

Answer
Option 1: *This option is correct. Role models mirror traits that you admire and want for yourself. Identifying these traits can help you iden-*

tify your values.

Option 2: *This option is correct. Family has a profound shaping effect on children's attitudes and behaviors.*

Option 3: *This option is correct. Your cultural teachings and expectations help shape your attitudes and behaviors.*

Option 4: *This option is correct. Peers play a large role in the formation of attitudes and core beliefs.*

Option 5: *This option is incorrect. You must know what your core beliefs are before you can transform any negative ones.*

Option 6: *This option is incorrect. Raising your children in a way that fosters the formation of positive core beliefs is something you should do, but it doesn't help you identify your own core beliefs.*

Identifying your biases

In addition to core values and core beliefs, another bit of important self-knowledge is your biases.

A **bias** is an unreasoned judgment that you make about a person. Bias is closely related to prejudice, which is a negative opinion or attitude formed without sufficient knowledge of a person or group of people.

Biases are destructive because they prevent people from reaching their full potential. And they choke off creativity and stifle the synergy that can occur when people of different knowledge levels and abilities work together.

To identify your own biases, you must start by observing your thoughts. Reflect on those around you. What thoughts, feelings, and mental pictures come to mind as you consider the people in your environment? If your thoughts are negative in any way, you might be biased. If that's the case, you need to analyze your thinking by digging deeper than the observation level.

To get an idea of how you should approach thought analysis, project yourself into each situation. Be sure to pay attention to your thoughts:

You're working with some sales people from another region. You note that they don't ever seem to hurry. You think, "I can't believe these people are so laid back."

An executive from the Finance Department is at your meeting. The person speaks in a loud tone of voice and starts pounding the table to make a point. You think, "All those people in Finance are so arrogant."

Several experienced people have left your department, and they have been replaced with new workers. The new workers aren't very skilled yet, and they slow you down. You think, "Why am I surrounded by incompetents?"

See each situation to learn about analyzing your thoughts.

Sales person
Ask yourself, "If the sales people had been from my area of the country, would I have had the same reaction?" If not, you may be displaying bias.

Executive
Ask yourself, "If this person weren't from Finance, would I have been so annoyed?" If the answer is no, you may be biased against people from this particular department.

New workers
Ask yourself, "If these people were more experienced, would I have thought of them as incompetent?" If the answer is no, you may have a bias against the new workers coming into your department.

To uncover your biases, examine your thinking. If your thoughts or feelings indicate you may have a bias, dig deeper and analyze those thoughts. Ask questions that can help you determine whether bias truly exists.

Question
John, a more experienced aide in a nursing home, watches a new aide struggle to set up portable X-ray equipment. John thinks, "They're not very well trained today, are they?"
Which question can John ask himself to determine whether he's biased?
Options:
1. "If the aide was more experienced, would I have assumed her

training was inadequate?"
2. "Should I ignore the aide's lack of skills?"
3. "Why can't we hire people who know what they're doing?"
Answer

Option 1: *This is the correct option. Because the aide is inexperienced, John assumes her training is inadequate. He has a bias against new workers.*

Option 2: *This option is incorrect. Ignoring the woman's lack of skills won't resolve John's dilemma. He needs to determine whether his thinking reveals a bias.*

Option 3: *This option is incorrect. Asking this question won't help John figure out whether he's guilty of bias.*

Managing diversity

When you're aware of your own values, core beliefs, and biases, you're equipped to manage your reactions in difficult situations involving diversity. One technique for doing this is to **take control of your self-talk**.

Your mind sends you messages all the time, relentlessly. Self-talk is the little voice in your head that you hear as you experience things and interact with people.

When self-talk is positive, your attitude is also positive. But when self-talk is negative, you can feel defeated and powerless. For example, it's much easier to recover from a mistake when you tell yourself, "I'll get some help next time and do better" than when you say "I'm so stupid. I knew I'd do it wrong." By learning to manage your self-talk, you can change the internal messages from negative to positive ones. It's a useful technique for dealing with your own and other's diversity.

Meet Martin. Martin is an IT worker for a large insurance company. When the Internet revolution hit his company, Martin struggled. He was three years from retirement and needed to keep his job. But he wasn't confident he could learn new skills, or that he'd be able to work with his new colleagues.

Follow along as Martin reveals how learning to manage his self-talk helped him out of his dilemma.

When the new technology started spreading through the company, I was scared. I told myself that I might be too old to learn computers. Then, when the influx of new people in my department began, I knew I was doomed. I was angry.

These newcomers looked at me like I was ready for the organizational trash heap. I didn't want to have anything to do with them. But I had to keep my job, or I wouldn't be able to retire with full benefits. So I decided to sign up for training classes. After the first class, I told my story to the instructor, Charlene. Charlene informed me that it's not my age that's holding me back – it's my attitude.

My negative self-talk was sabotaging my ability to move forward. After working one-on-one with Charlene for a while, I realized that learning the new technology was no more difficult than other challenges I'd faced. I also realized that my life experience could be very helpful to some of my new colleagues. In the end, it wasn't easy, but it worked out. My coworkers and I maintain a give-and-take of skills and knowledge that I really enjoy. We have a mutual respect, which helps to smooth out the misunderstandings that sometimes occur.

By replacing his negative messages with positive ones, Martin changed his attitude about himself and his new coworkers. He continues to use positive self-talk to keep himself moving forward.

In addition to helping you deal with people who have different views, self-talk is useful for coping with feelings of anger and frustration and for dealing with people from different cultures.

So, self-talk is useful. But how do you work on your self-talk? You can follow three steps. First, you must identify your internal messages. Next, challenge them. And finally, replace the negative messages with positive, rational ones.

See each step to learn more about it.

Identify internal messages

Your first step in dealing with self-talk is to acknowledge and identify it. You need to isolate the internal messages that are critical of you and others.

For example, if you're working on a tough problem, do you hear, "I'll figure it out. I'm good at this." Or do you hear, "I'm too stupid to figure this out"? This last message is the kind you need to identify.

Challenge negative self-talk

Challenge any self-talk messages that are inaccurate, exaggerated, or defeating.

For example, if you hear a message like "I'll never finish this thing on time," ask yourself, "Am I exaggerating the problem?" "Am I being too hard on myself?" or "Is this rational?" Or if the self-talk is about others, ask "Am I being biased?"

Replace negative messages with positive ones

Rewrite your self-talk. If you hear "I can't do this; I'm going to fail," substitute the message with "I'm taking it one step at a time, and I'll get it right."

Consider Trudi. Trudi is a buyer at a department store. She selects clothing for clients and takes it to their homes for them to try on. Many of her clients are from different countries. One client in particular, Mrs. Fisher, is always late. This really upsets Trudi because, to her, time is money. Trudi thinks, "This woman doesn't respect me; I wouldn't do this to her" and "I'm going to end my working relationship with her."

If Trudi acts on her self-talk, she'll lose a client, and the client may take other clients with her. Fortunately, Trudi becomes conscious of her self-talk. Follow along as she finds another way to approach the situation.

> I can't go on thinking these negative thoughts. They're coloring all of my interactions with this woman.
>
> I wonder if I'm exaggerating or being irrational. I don't have any evidence that Mrs. Fisher is aware that her lateness is upsetting me.
>
> The best solution is to talk to Mrs. Fisher.

When Trudi talks to Mrs. Fisher, the woman is very surprised. In her culture, people perceive time differently, and showing up late isn't a sign of disrespect. By challenging her self-talk, Trudi was able to clarify the misunderstanding and strengthen her relationship with Mrs. Fisher.

Question

Your manager is from a different cultural background, and he's a hard taskmaster. He highlights your shortcomings, but never praises your achievements. At first, his behavior made you nervous. Now, though, you're angry.
Whenever you come into contact with your manager, you think, "There he goes, spreading misery. I wish he'd go back to wherever he came from." Eventually, the very presence of your manager makes you queasy.
Which is the most appropriate way for you to manage your self-talk?

Options:

1. Acknowledge you're doing it, and pinpoint which messages are negative ones 2. Challenge the negative self-talk
3. Exchange the negative self-talk for positive self-talk
4. Understand that everyone has a different management style
5. Talk to coworkers about your feelings and ask for their advice

Answer

Option 1: *This option is correct. The first step in turning around the self-talk is to acknowledge you're doing it and identify which messages are negative.*

Option 2: *This option is correct. Challenge your negativity. Ask yourself, "Is the boss really evil? In his own mind, he's just doing his job."*

Option 3: *This option is correct. Instead of thinking, "There he goes, spreading misery," you might think, "There goes a man who has the ability to manage people who don't share his cultural background or beliefs."*

Option 4: *This option is incorrect. This may soothe you to a small degree, but it won't help you manage self-talk.*

Option 5: *This option is incorrect. Coworkers can't help you manage your own self-talk, and complaining can make negativity worse.*

Summary

Self-awareness can determine how successful you are when working with diverse people. The elements you need to be able to identify are your core values, core beliefs, and biases.

Values are the overriding principles that guide your actions and behaviors. Such things as duty, honor, family, and security define how you make your decisions each day. Core beliefs are truths that you hold about yourself. They're not universal truths, but truths as you believe them to be. Biases are unreasoned judgments you make about others. Values, core beliefs, and biases often have their roots in your upbringing.

One way to take charge of your interactions with other people is to manage your self-talk. You can do this in three steps: identify the negative messages, challenge them, and replace them with positive ones.

EMBRACING DIVERSITY

Be open to change
The Greek philosopher Heraclitus once said, "The only constant in life is change." Although people build their lives on the idea of predictability, very little in life is truly predictable. If you try to cling to old attitudes, ideas, and behaviors, you'll become isolated.

Question
How are you at handling change? Are you able to adapt your attitudes and behaviors as you learn new things about the world?
Options:
1. I'm not very adaptable 2. I'm working on it
3. I'm very adaptable
Answer
Option 1: *Well, change is hard. Many people have difficulty with it. This course will help you learn about adapting to change.*
Option 2: *Good! Life is easier when you can adapt your behaviors and attitudes and go with the flow. This course will help you learn about adapting to change.*
Option 3: *Great! This is a good attitude to have for learning to deal with diversity in your workplace. This course will help you learn about adapting to change.*

To embrace diversity, you must be open to change. In this topic, you'll learn about tips for improving your awareness of intercultural differences, as well as improving your ability to deal with differences among people.

This is important to both you and your organization. When you're able to fully embrace diversity yourself, you'll be in a good position to work with others in the organization whose viewpoints differ from yours. You'll be helping to unlock the creativity and innovation necessary for you and your organization to thrive.

To learn more about embracing diversity, these methods are a good place to start:

develop a nuanced world view

assume there are no strange behaviors, just behaviors you don't yet understand be willing to set aside your own standards when thinking of different cultures, and be an advocate for diversity

Develop a nuanced world view

One method for embracing diversity is to **develop a nuanced world view**. As you begin to achieve self-awareness by exploring your core values and beliefs, you'll learn that your perspectives are only relative, and not the universal truths you may have thought them to be.

In fact, there are very few totally right or wrong perspectives. If you can adopt this thinking, you'll gain a truer picture of people and events. Having a nuanced view of the world, however, makes it more difficult to navigate. Just as nothing is really right or wrong, very few behaviors are clear-cut.

Question

To correctly interpret the behaviors and actions of others, you must unlearn or ignore some of the actions that come naturally to you.

Which do you think you should unlearn?

Options:
1. The habit of judging based on first impressions
2. Judging others by their actions
3. Looking beyond superficial behaviors
4. Judging people by what they do rather than what they say

Answer

Option 1: This option is correct. First impressions are terribly misleading. They cause you to judge people by superficial qualities such as

age, gender, and ethnicity.
Option 2: *This option is correct. People from different cultural backgrounds may behave in ways that are quite different from your norms. Judging people based on their differences can keep you from knowing who they really are.*
Option 3: *This option is incorrect. This is a behavior you need to practice, not unlearn. You*
must look beyond the initial superficial impression of people's behaviors.
Option 4: *This option is incorrect. Actually, you should replace judgment with curiosity and not judge at all.*

If you want to correctly interpret the behaviors of others, you must avoid judging people on their first impressions and stop judging people's behaviors according to your own standards. Learn to take time to figure out what's really happening.
Consider this. When Marve met Tupak at their sister company in another country, Marve's first reaction was unfavorable. Why? When the two men shook hands, Tupak's grasp was very soft, and he held onto Marve's hand for a long time. Marve mistook Tupak's gentleness for weakness. Later, after meeting more people, Marve realized that Tupak's handshake was standard in his country. Marve learned an important lesson – don't jump to conclusions.

Investigate unusual behaviors
A second method for learning to embrace diversity is to make the assumption that **there are no strange behaviors, just behaviors you don't yet understand**.
Learning more about why people act the way they do can help you avoid misunderstandings. A good plan for investigating the behaviors of others is to first acknowledge that the behavior makes sense to the other person. Second, question yourself about what the behavior could mean. Finally, ask the person, or someone from the same background, what the behavior actually means.
Sandra and Tai are engineers who are working together on an in-

ternational project. When Sandra asked Tai to help her out with some administrative tasks, Tai became quite upset and walked away from her.

Sandra was angry, so she confronted Tai. It turns out that, in Tai's culture, asking professionals to perform administrative tasks is insulting. But the damage was done. Sandra's confrontational attitude had angered Tai.

The problem could've been avoided if Sandra had **acknowledged that Tai's behavior made sense to him**. She could have found a different, calmer, and more appropriate approach to use.

The second step in investigating unusual behavior is to **question yourself about what the behavior might mean**.

For example, Laura works with Ken, who recently emigrated from another country. Although she's excited to be working with Ken, Laura quickly becomes frustrated. She's direct and to the point. Ken is very reserved and seems reluctant to offer specifics about his opinions or thinking. Laura steps back and asks herself, "Do I offend Ken without knowing it? Why doesn't he offer ideas or criticisms of my ideas?"

After observing Ken's interactions with others and reading about his native culture, Laura understands. People in Ken's culture are reserved, polite, and use a circular style of discussion rather than a direct, head-on style. Understanding helps Laura alter her style to accommodate her new coworker.

Now, if you can't figure out why someone is behaving in a way that seems strange to you, **ask the person, or someone from the same background, what the behavior means**.

Francois notices that one of his coworkers, Jean-Marc, disappears from the office several times a day, always at the same time of day. Francois is curious, but he doesn't know Jean-Marc well and doesn't want to offend him. Francois asks Marie-Andre, a friend of Jean-Marc's, what's going on.

Marie-Andre explains that Jean-Marc is very devout, and prays several times a day. Jean-Marc leaves the work area so he can find privacy.

Question
A good way to save yourself embarrassment and get a head start on embracing diversity is to educate yourself in the cultural and social norms of different cultures.
Which methods do you think you can use to increase your cultural literacy?
Options:
1. Films
2. Books
3. Discussions with friends from other cultures 4. Questionnaires
5. Crossword puzzles
Answer
Option 1: *This option is correct. Films are an excellent way to learn about other cultures.* **Option 2:** *This option is correct. Both nonfiction and fiction books are good ways to learn*
about people from other cultures.
Option 3: *This option is correct. If you have the opportunity to talk with friends about their culture, this is a great way to learn more.*
Option 4: *This option is incorrect. Questionnaires can't really impart understanding about other people's cultures.*
Option 5: *This option is incorrect. You can't really learn much about other people's cultures from doing crossword puzzles.*

Attend film screenings, read books, and have conversations with friends to learn how other people live. You'll find out about some important basic differences, including how people communicate, how they think about time, how they deal with conflict, and their views toward individualism versus collectivism.
See each cultural difference to learn more.

Communication
In some cultures, things are spelled out explicitly. People depend on instructions and directions that are spoken or written down. Contrast this with a culture in which people depend on shared knowledge. Less is spelled out explicitly, and much more is implicit or communicated indirectly.

Time considerations

In some cultures, time is perceived as a limited resource that's constantly being used up. Time is money. It can be sliced, scheduled, and wasted. Meetings begin at the appointed hour.

In other cultures, time is more fluid. Meetings begin when everyone gets there, and it's not as important if meetings exceed their scheduled duration.

Dealing with conflict

In some cultures, conflict is to be avoided, and preserving good relationships and harmony is all-important.

In other cultures, problems are tackled head-on, and people openly confront each other.

Individualism vs collectivism

In individualist cultures, people want autonomy. A person is admired for being "self-made" and making decisions independently. In collectivist cultures, however, people identify with and work well in groups. Individualism is frowned upon.

Set aside your behavior standards

In addition to developing a nuanced world view and investigating behaviors that seem strange to you, a third step toward embracing diversity is to **set aside your standards** when dealing with diverse people. Develop empathy and replace your judgments with curiosity.

Empathy is the ability to identify with others and sympathize with their situations. It involves the heart, as well as the mind. Some people are able to empathize naturally and easily. Others must learn how. To learn how to empathize, practice using three techniques:
- suspend your judgment
- set aside your perspective, and
- communicate your understanding to the other person

See each step for more information.

Suspend judgment

Don't judge the person or the situation. Instead, allow your natural curiosity to guide you. Tell yourself, "I genuinely want to understand this person."

Set aside perspective
Set aside your own perspective and put yourself in the other person's position. "Walk a mile in the person's shoes" as the saying goes. What does it feel like? What are you thinking?

Communicate understanding
Let the other person know that you understand or that you want to understand the person's position. Say something like "I can imagine how difficult this is for you." Be sure to back up your words with nonverbal communication. The look on your face, the openness in your body position, and the tone of your voice are as important as what you say.

Be a diversity advocate
And finally, when you've become confident in your ability to handle situations involving diversity, the final step in embracing diversity is to **become a diversity advocate**. Be the solution – the person that others go to for guidance in difficult situations.

As a diversity advocate, you'll have a lot to do – bridging differences and building understanding, helping coworkers become more comfortable with diversity, and discussing cultural differences behind different behaviors.

See each action to learn more about it.

Bridge differences and build understanding
As a diversity advocate, you should become a cultural interpreter for others. Help people come together by understanding each other's behaviors.

Help coworkers become more comfortable
Become knowledgeable about the backgrounds of people around you and spread your knowledge of other people's backgrounds, beliefs, and cultures.

Discuss cultural differences
Find opportunities to build understanding of people from other backgrounds and cultures. If you hear a disparaging comment

about a colleague, take the time to explain to the speaker that the colleague's behavior isn't odd in that person's culture.

Question

To embrace diversity, you must first understand the cultural and social diversity in your workplace.

Which are guidelines for doing this?

Options:

1. Understand the nuances of behavior and avoid perceiving things as all good or all bad
2. Put yourself in the shoes of others and try to understand the behavior from their perspective
3. Replace judgment with curiosity
4. Become a source of information about diversity in your workplace
5. Help people with different backgrounds finish their work
6. Target people who are different from you for friendship

Answer

Option 1: This option is correct. Behavior is complex and multilayered. You need to perceive it in all its nuances and avoid thinking in terms of right or wrong, or good or bad.

Option 2: This option is correct. Behavior that seems strange to you is probably normal to people from other backgrounds. Investigate different behaviors rather than judge them.

Option 3: This option is correct. Set aside your behavior standards and tell yourself that you really want to understand the other person. Develop empathy.

Option 4: This option is correct. After you've been able to embrace diversity yourself, it's important to become a diversity advocate.

Option 5: This option is not correct. Finishing the work of others won't help spread diversity. ***Option 6:*** *This option is not correct. Understanding someone from another culture may lead to*
friendship, but friendship doesn't necessarily lead to embracing diversity.

Summary

Embracing diversity may require you to change your attitudes, beliefs, and behaviors. To practice doing this, follow four steps.

First, develop a nuanced world view. Avoid thinking of other people's behaviors as all good or all bad. Second, suspend judgment. Don't think of the behavior of others as strange just because it's new to you.

Third, set aside your behavior standards. Other people behave differently – accept their behaviors without comparing them to your own preconceived notions of what's proper. Educate yourself about other cultures.

Finally, become a diversity advocate. After you've learned to embrace diversity yourself, become an advocate for diversity throughout your organization.

COMMUNICATING IN A DIVERSE SETTING

The most important tool
The most important tool you have for building rapport with others is **communication**. But communication can be tricky in diverse organizations, where people have different attitudes, behaviors, and values. For instance, ask yourself these questions: "How will I know that others understand me?" "How much detail should I give?" "How much background can I assume my listeners have?" "Should I tell a joke to break the ice?" "Should I be formal or informal in my manner?"
Fortunately, you can follow guidelines to help minimize the risk of miscommunication and help create an inclusive climate. These guidelines concern three aspects of communication: your style, the way you listen, and your verbal and nonverbal language.

Be flexible about your style
Reflect
Think about your own communication style.
Are you direct and to the point? Or are you indirect and circular? Are you detailed and specific? Or are you general and open ended? Do you like to tell jokes or use interesting metaphors? Or are you more formal?

When it comes to communication, one size definitely doesn't fit all. A style that's direct and to the point can alienate those who need a more indirect approach. A conversation full of sports references will turn off people who aren't interested in sports. And if you like to tell jokes, tread carefully. Humor is highly subjective and can cause offense in an instant.

The most important guideline when it comes to your communication style is to **be flexible**. To be effective in a diverse environment, you have to adjust your style to the people you're speaking with. You should take into consideration all aspects that make the person an individual.
Adjusting your style isn't always easy. But you can learn to do it if you're mindful of others' needs and use a series of steps:
1. make a list of people at work you deal with the most
2. analyze their communication style
3. determine how to improve your compatibility with them, and
4. implement needed changes
See each step, in order, to learn more.

1. Make a list of people at work you deal with the most
You can't possibly accommodate everyone, but you can adapt your style to people you work with every day. So make a list of who those people are.

2. Analyze their communication style
Go down the list and determine how you should communicate with each person. For example, does the list contain anyone of a different ethnicity who may require a different style?

3. Determine how to improve your compatibility with them
Depending on what different people need in step two, decide what you must do to communicate better.

4. Implement changes
Incorporate your ideas from step three when you communicate with each individual. If you know the person well, you may want to ask for feedback so that you can improve even more.

Remember, when you adapt your style to others' needs, you make it easier for people to understand you. You're better able to be a good communicator in a diverse environment.

Practice active listening

A second guideline for communicating in a diverse setting is to **practice active listening**. Listening is an important skill in any environment, but especially in a diverse environment.

You'll face many obstacles to effective listening in a diverse environment. For example, your attitude about the speaker could prevent you from hearing what's being said. You may be listening only for facts rather than the speaker's underlying meaning. Or you could be focusing on how the speaker looks and sounds, thereby missing the shades of meaning. It's very easy to misunderstand others from different cultures and backgrounds.

You may be able to prevent most misunderstandings if you follow some **guidelines for active listening**. To be an active listener, perform these specific actions:
- suspend judgment
- listen carefully
  check understanding by paraphrasing, and
- ask questions if you don't understand

Active listening actually helps the speaker learn to communicate better. By following active listening techniques, you're teaching the speaker how to communicate with you in the style that works best for you.

Question
Which statements are correct about active listening?
Options:
1. Active listening requires you to ask questions if you don't understand the speaker
2. Your attitude toward the speaker can prevent you from understanding what the speaker is saying
3. Active listening requires you to suspend judgment of the speaker
4. With active listening, you should paraphrase what you've heard to check your understanding
5. Active listening requires learning about the backgrounds of the people you speak with every day
6. Your attitude toward active listening can affect the

style of the speaker

Answer

Option 1: *This option is correct. When you listen actively, you have a part to play in the communication. If you don't understand something, ask the speaker for clarification.*

Option 2: *This option is correct. You may have some biases that prevent you from listening to and understanding the speaker.*

Option 3: *This option is correct. You can't listen if you're busy judging the speaker or the style in which the information is being delivered.*

Option 4: *This option is correct. Paraphrasing allows you to check your understanding and correct any misimpressions.*

Option 5: *This option is incorrect. You can practice active listening without knowing the background of the speaker.*

Option 6: *This option is incorrect. As an active listener, you help the speaker communicate with you. Your attitude toward active listening is immaterial.*

Use inclusive language

The third guideline for communicating in a diverse environment is to **use inclusive language**. Language shapes reality, and you must choose your words and phrases carefully to include everyone in this reality.

For instance, it's surprising how many people assume others understand their slang, sports references, and colorful metaphors. The fact is, many people don't understand, and using this kind of language excludes them from the discussion.

Meet Sean. Sean is a lawyer with an American engineering company. He received an urgent call from a client in England. Sean had faxed a contract to the client for his signature, with a note that he needed the client's "John Hancock" – American slang for "signature." The client was very confused because John Hancock hadn't been involved in the contract negotiations, and he wanted this person brought into the discussions immediately.

Sean was embarrassed, and the misunderstanding was quickly cleared up. But Sean could've easily avoided the whole issue in the first place. If he'd used a little common sense, Sean would've known that his English client wouldn't get the reference to an American patriot who lived in the eighteenth century.

The point is to think before you speak. Use language that doesn't exclude anyone from understanding your meaning. What this means is that you must not make assumptions about what others know, you must use gender-neutral language, you should avoid using culturally specific metaphors, and you must avoid slang.

See each guideline to learn more about avoiding noninclusive language.

Avoid assumptions about what others know

Some experiences are so overwhelming that they create a common reference. However, there are very few experiences that are like that. So be very careful about what you assume others know. People from other cultures won't have any idea what you mean if you refer to the ride of Paul Revere or even the Super Bowl.

Use gender-neutral language

If you use language that refers to males as the dominant gender, you exclude over half of the population.

So when you refer to all human beings, use "humanity," not "mankind." Use terms such as
"chairperson" instead of "chairman." Avoid prefacing an occupational title with the person's gender – woman doctor, woman firefighter, or female supervisor could cause offense.

Avoid culturally specific metaphors

Metaphors are powerful figures of speech that convey meaning to people who share common knowledge or experiences. However, in a diverse workplace, metaphors prevent many people from understanding your message.

If you use language like "three strikes and you're out," for example, some members of your audience simply won't know what you mean.

Avoid slang

Slang is pervasive in many cultures. Try to avoid slang, because it's very culture-specific. For instance, if someone said to you "The escalator is broken; use the apple and pears," would you know what to do?

New slang expressions enter languages all the time, so be careful. If you refer to coworkers as your "peeps," don't be surprised when you get blank stares in return.

Using inclusive language is imperative. Doing so helps to ensure understanding and fosters an environment in which everyone feels valued and equal as a contributor. Do your best to eliminate obstacles to understanding – be mindful about slang, metaphors, common assumptions, and potentially derogatory language.

Question

Which statements include examples of noninclusive language?
Options:
1. "The vice president of purchasing will be attending our meeting, so we need to get our ducks in a row."
2. "Maya needs to improve her performance; she's got two strikes against her already."
3. "Our new CD will be produced by the big shots at the recording studio."
4. "We ought to congratulate ourselves; the customer loved the presentation."
5. "If we leave now, we'll all make it back to our offices in time for the conference call."

Answer

Option 1: *This option is correct. Instead of talking about "getting ducks in a row," this person could have talked about "coordinating our efforts," which means the same thing.*
Option 2: *This option is correct. Would someone from a different culture know that Maya has one chance left? Likely not. Sports metaphors are noninclusive.*
Option 3: *This option is correct. "the big shots" makes this statement non-inclusive. This is slang which could be misunderstood, it would be better to use the word "people" instead.*
Option 4: *This option is incorrect. There are no obstacles to understanding in this statement. The language is plain and inclusive.*

Option 5: *This option is incorrect. The language is inclusive, and this statement contains no obstacles to understanding.*

Summary

Communication is your most important tool for dealing with diversity in the workplace. And it's one of the most difficult things to master. You can use certain guidelines for handling communication.

First, be flexible in your communication style. Rather than stick with the style that suits you, consider how you may need to adapt your style to suit the people you speak with.

Next, practice active listening. Make eye contact with the speaker, listen carefully, summarize, and ask questions to ensure you understand the message being sent.

Finally, use inclusive, gender-neutral language. And avoid slang, humor, or metaphors that could be culture-specific or offensive.

www.ingramcontent.com/pod-product-compliance
Lightning Source LLC
Chambersburg PA
CBHW070853220526
45466CB00005B/1974